Search Party

Richard Meier was born in Surrey in 1970. He won the inaugural Picador Poetry Prize in 2010 and his first collection, *Misadventure*, was published by Picador in 2012. He works in mental health and relationship support policy, and lives in north London with his wife, daughter and son.

ALSO BY RICHARD MEIER

Misadventure

Richard Meier

Search Party

PICADOR

First published 2019 by Picador
an imprint of Pan Macmillan
20 New Wharf Road, London N1 9RR
Associated companies throughout the world
www.panmacmillan.com

ISBN 978-1-5098-5198-0

A CIP catalogue record for this book is available from the British Library.

Printed and bound by CPI Group (UK) Ltd, Croydon, CR0 4YY

Visit **www.picador.com** to read more about all our books
and to buy them. You will also find features, author interviews and
news of any author events, and you can sign up for e-newsletters
so that you're always first to hear about our new releases.

For Matilda and Wilf

Contents

Search Party

At a porcelain collection

Among the flasks and vases,
cobalt koi and dragons,
the stillest of still things:

five *plain, domestic bowls,
circa 1300.*
Unhandled, never filled,

what life for them without
that one life-giving thing –
the possibility of breaking?

Last chance

What are you doing, Daddy? asks the boy
discovering his father in the long, west-facing garden.
Just sitting in the sun, he answers, sketchily –

it's too soon for his three-year-old to face
I'm savouring the last bit of the light, and so on.
What are you doing now? the boy asks some time later,

the sun-patch less an oblong than a square,
though soon, in truth, rectangular again,
but crossways now, a slab across the garden.

And when the boy returns he calls out
Why are you standing there against the wall, Daddy?
then *Why are you standing on that chair?*

The achievement of naturalism in Greek sculpture

Hair, of course, was a long-standing joke.
They knew, these makers, that it neither falls
in beads nor tidy rivulets; still,
no matter – symmetry was all they cared for.
Imagine then their shock

when one among them cast a bronze whose weight
sat firmly on its back leg, stood with hips
at different levels, and whose head was turned
a little to one side. Hooked by such aliveness,
they couldn't help but notice that the slight

twist which the head-turn set off in the body
was not quite reflected in the torso; worse,
they saw that their replacement of the dumb,
Egyptian non-grin with a smile showed simply
how lifeless was the face in general.

How could it prove so hard, becoming truer,
they'd wonder, each advance exposing
fresh forms of awkwardness? Why could they not revert
to what they knew, that plain, un-weathering look?
What on earth had they begun?

Hell

Though real to me,
my fear of things
is not a 'thing',
the dictionary
of phobias suggests.

Strange, since a fear
of things on one's left
is accorded a name,
as is a fear
of those to one's right.

Perhaps it's a strain
of taphephobia –
where rather than terror
of being interred
under earth,

alive, the fear's
not of mud but of stuff.
Re-reading the list,
I find that some
might be paired:

chiraptophobia (fear
of being touched)
and chirophobia
(of hands), for example.
Poor loves.

And then, how fitting
that genio-, geno-
and genu-phobias
(chins, sex and knees)
come in that order.

Not that it's funny,
of course. Consider,
a moment, these:
the anthrophobic,
afraid of flowers;

the cardiophobic,
they who are cursed
with a fear of the heart;
optophobes, loath
to open their eyes.

Porto Maurizio

(a homage)

Stepping diagonally
like a bishop,
bedroom to hallway, lounge
to kitchen, as this storey
was once – for some good reason
lost to us – arranged,
you come out on the balcony.

Facing it, one owner
has lashed an awning (always drawn)
across theirs, while another
has pitched an ugly glass
and aluminium porch.
The walls are shaded pastel, naturally,
ochre or peach, or neither.

Pot plants watch over any number
of ways of hanging washing,
while various pipes, put in
post hoc, emerge like surprises.
A vision in heuristics –
a mish-mash, not a symphony.
(As near a creed
as one might wish to get.)

The Flight

after Ovid

Whispering, banknotes, handshake: some big plan
his father — all the boy has, since the shelling —
is taking care of. Yes, if anyone
will get them out of here, then *he* will.
Keep to the middle of the boat, his father tells him,
hands trembling while he helps his young son in.
Yet by the time this boat-raw boy sees land
and rushes to that side, along with the others,
those words have melted and the boat's
half-under — so this man, no more a father,
will cry out in the water for his son,
then by the water's edge, until
the boy is spotted, towards evening —
the bedclothes of the shallows pulled up close around him.

Snow

The pavement/road distinction softened early on;
and soon enough one shrub looked much like any other.

A few things seemed to gain, however: garden chairs,
for instance, showing off their plump, pristine new cushions.

And still it snowed, till gross shapes only
defined the simplifying world.

This is more like it! all the tall things crowed,
their voices shrill, then shriller,

as if they now could never come,
the thaw, the colour.

On the looting of museums

for Verity

To learn from one another,
to grow, we have to risk
sharing antiquities, risk
their loss, theft or destruction,
says my curator friend,
remarkably, I feel,
for someone so devoted.

And I think of what of mine
is out on loan with you;
and likewise what of yours
I harbour in return.
But, more, what rarer, frailer
pieces I might entrust to your
deep care, and vice versa,

that our two cultures even closer grow.

Findings

i
Lullaby

Five hundred parents from a Midwest state
are quizzed on *if*, and if so, *how*
a baby can be spoiled.

It turns out almost one in ten,
yes, one in ten, believe
that this can happen if

a baby's either rocked or held –
yes, rocked or held,
rocked or held.

ii
From an infant observation

Suspended in his racing-car-styled walker –
even on tip-toes just too tall for him –
he does not cry. A sound comes from the kitchen.

He beats the plastic dashboard with his fists,
but does not cry. So it is nearly done,
this learning to make do without soft things.

Ask him in years to come about his childhood
and he will answer, *It was fine. Why?* or
I really don't remember very much.

iii
Live company

A baby moves a mouse upon a table.
On one screen (linked up to the mouse) a cursor
mimics her movements perfectly; on a second,

a cursor guided by a person gives
a rough approximation only of her gestures.
And guess which one this baby, every baby, looks to?

Yes, who would choose mere echo,
pure agreement, over the game, the other,
the nearly-but-not-quiteness, life?

iv
State of nature

Abraham G., Earl H. and Donald R.,
three babies who, for the first half
of nineteen twenty-seven, are allowed

to choose – from "cereals, meat and seafood,
bone marrow, eggs, fruit, vegetables and salt" –
what food they eat. And the result?

They neither gorge themselves
on the richer, sweeter stuff, nor starve.
Free to discover what they know, they thrive.

Still Face Experiment

A mum sits opposite her baby, cooing
and playing normally. Then she goes like stone.
And what the baby makes of all of this,

how it responds, is noted down.
And this is okay, since it's taking place
under prescribed conditions, and just once.

I mean, it's not as if it's going on
undocumented, time and time again,
not in a lab but, say, a kitchen.

Raynaud's

All colour from the fingers,
the palms, wrists, forearms even.
Burning cold. And the toes.

The heart, pragmatic always,
electing to withdraw
warmth from the farthest reaches.

A flowering in reverse,
a bulb I am become,
arms wrapped tight like skin.

The question game

Sometimes, driving home,
we'll play the question game
and tot up what we have been asked,
that afternoon or weekend, in return.
One point for a *How are you?*
For anything more particular, two.

To love is to enquire, no?
we'd reason, though would say
As long as we're well, they're happy,
to mask the poorness of the score.
Then fall to staring at the soft, dun fields
holding the motorway, and the horizon.

The present

The shops are shutting. I've left it too late
to buy you any kind of gift
that might mean something. When we die,

when we admit we had time, in our lives,
to be with people more particularly,
to see them, let them know that they are seen,

but didn't, will it feel like this,
I wonder, weighing up
the corner shop, its chocolates, its closed roses.

End of the war story

One minute to eleven
when Private Henry Gunther –
American,
if German by descent –
is waved back
from a roadblock,
yet he – demoted
two months earlier
for a silly thing,
and smarting –
feels no peace
and keeps on
coming

Tipping point

Seven and six, the children now;
I wonder, crouched behind the crisp-thin, rusty wheelbarrow,
is this the last game of hide and seek we'll ever play?

Footsteps approach – *Where is he?* they confer –
and then recede; come close again, recede
once more, then nothing. Minutes fall.

I should come out, I think, in case they're worried.
Unless they have moved on to something else,
are not worried at all?

On the soul

We speak of *soul-destroying* –
as if we name a process,
yet one which has no end;

as if the soul
were inexhaustible

or else comes with the power
to self-replenish, auto-nourish,

but is it, does it?

The art of the through ball

Easy ball! yell his team-mates who would rather
he play it to where someone's already standing
than try what might, if read, be beautiful –
the desolate pass to open a defence,
that's slid to no one, into emptiness

Christmas scene

A large, or quite large, red balloon,
left over from a child's birthday,
is being batted round a living room
by generations of a family,
the main aim being to keep it in the air
while making sure to not let it explode
which, with holly everywhere
and other piercing things, is hard
though not impossible, it would appear,
so deftly bypassed are the obstacles,
so long is the balloon saved from the floor,
the youngest of the boys and girls
following each move of those who are showing
what love can look like, as they keep it going

Helicopters

Room on our flight-deck for just one,
what could we do but wave them in, in turn,
and help the people off – South Vietnamese,
of course, these pilots and their families –
then start to push the things, barge
them edgewards till, with a slow tipping, like huge
mantises turning into whales, they'd slide
right into the loose South China Sea. I'm told
they had flown beyond the point of no return
to find us. As each helicopter drowned,
I felt time tighten, as though plunge-cooled
to form fact and history at the point where all
these hopes and these griefs I had no right
to witness – and luck – touched.

Presentiment

And if you two should meet,
and strip to your lacquered skins –
for why, like richer qualities,
should not emptiness seek its twin? –

then all that will be heard
is the knock of each outermost shell
of Matryoshka man
on Matryoshka doll.

Things people said when I lost an eye

include *At least you haven't lost an arm.*
And though they had a point, I guess,
I took the statement more to mean
Something's befallen you I cannot face.

Medical science is developing every year
was another. Something I took to signal
how hard they found it, not being able to help.
No matter, I've said clumsier things.

And besides, I had a good friend,
one who could tell me, *Rich, you've lost an eye,*
so I could hear. And a mother who could say,
I'm sorry, I'm so sorry.

Boy

i
Day-old

Not that I thought he'd be exempt, you realise.
Still, as I left the hospital that evening,
it rankled, how the world had shown no give
whatever, had simply carried on.

So, you're taking him too?
I may even have muttered –
a comment meant, of course, for *time*,
whose hands feel gentle,

encouraging, as they guide and carry
before un-cupping, flattening,
so as to steer, to shove. I mean, no grace
at all, not a day, an hour even.

ii
First night home

Despite the rain, like gravel,
the gardensful of air hurled
at walls, forced down the brickwind
instrument of the chimney,
this house will not crumble.

We know this, yet we quail –
for we have brought home *fear*,
all bundled. And only
this aching, anchoring
vigilance for a shield.

iii
An eight-month-old during the London Olympics

Even the weather went for it –
the run-up to the games
the wettest, shiniest spring
since records began.

You, alone, refrained –
not for you, or not yet,
such childish things,
the besting and the strain;

the world as yet unordered –
like someone looking out from under a low lintel after rain,
you scan the whole expanse
from small ripe fist to the horizon

and find it fine,
and grin.

iv
The early years

Rest these days down
one above another –
these lucent, rhymed,
child-centred days –
and you might note
little difference;
look more closely
and you'll find
tiny changes
at the edges,
here or there
a double outline –
new words, phrases,
syntax, skills –
small, like errors,
such as scribes make;
as if, somehow,
our children know
the cost of each
small deviation,
and would replay
each day and yet,
despite themselves,
they learn, so leave us.

V
Precociousness

That look of pride/surprise
one parent gives the other
at what their child's done early

has loss, too, in one corner:
they'd time, they reckoned, still —
time with that overwritten child.

vi
Wouldn't we all

My four-year-old son: *Daddy –*
for my next birthday
I'd like a search party

Railroad Alaska

— the programme I'm half-watching
when you pad through,
complaining you can't sleep.

And as there's little
in it that might perturb
a six-year-old, I figure,

we huddle down
to follow the travails
of these half-frozen folk:

the driver of the train,
a policeman on a snowmobile,
an off-gridder named Jim,

who — *Daddy, is that real!?* —
has an actual hook for a hand.
Cut back to the train:

the driver's worried —
the policeman has discovered
a tree across the line —

he needs to get his freight,
a verst of silver rails,
to where they will replace

those fractured by the cold;
and Jim there in the carriage,
hugging a busted shoulder –

he's had another fall
and needs a doctor, bad.
Gregarious, curious child,

beyond the drama and the hook,
what will you make of this,
the night you stayed up with your father –

the fates of men so alien to you still,
these tableaux of remoteness,
these increments of withdrawal?

My dad, the astronaut

To think I cheered,
that morning in the desert,
watching the rocket
rocketing and so prove

that, unlike space,
love's circumscribed.
Right up to blast-off,
I thought he'd cry *Stop!*

Our fathers' clothes

The blues, reds, mauves of their V-necks and their polos –
when did they bleed to that slim, wan palette
of taupe and tan, shades of olive?

And when did they blanch, as if left in the sun,
these trousers, cardigans, slip-ons even –
to sand, to biscuit, barley, stone?

An old man dreams of rescuing his mother

Always a car, the same car,
same few roads; same urge
to intervene, to save the driver
for whom to change course
or to swerve would spell disaster;
or pull her from the vehicle
even though however deep
the water into which
the wreckage plunges, whatever
speed-times-tonnage she,
head-on, encounters,
she comes out quite unscathed,
a miracle, and he's the one trapped,
drowning, burning, maimed.

The answer

Where in the whole world would you like to be right now?
a girl I once liked asked me. Meaning me to say,
I think, *the Hindu Kush* or *Angkor Wat,*
not *It depends on who was there.*
Asked now, I'd answer
Norfolk
and mean its north-
easternmost, least entreating
scrap, mean its dunes, a sheet of paper torn
lengthways, then turned landscape; and here and there,
those pinnacled church towers, like long-eared owls, and you.

"Stocks of your blood group are falling"

(donor appeal following a terrorist attack)

O
negative:
the blood, I
always thought,
of those who cannot
tolerate that of another
kind. I understand now (yes,
I had to let an idea go) its very
ordinariness – it can be given
to anyone – is what is key.
It's indiscriminate,
in fact.

The daffodil

Pre-occupied, I guess, we left the bulbs
to winter on a low garden table.

Come March, a single daffodil
had shouldered through the opening of the bag to leave

a stew of barely opened buds beneath the plastic.
And I stood a moment, gob-smacked by the flower,

or more by what its blooming must have led to,
a realisation, as it grew and loosened,

of fundamental wrongness, some core shortfall
that must have nearly done for it,

for all the brass neck, all the yelling *yellow*.

On a new one-way system

as if the whole earth had been greased
some great agreement reached

as if this were a reasonable exchange
for speed – such breeziness

as if we could be suited to a world
with nothing oncoming

could be trusted to a sphere
where one cannot stop

as if we were a river

To a landlord

A small act, to brick up
the fireplace in a lounge
to let an extra bedroom.

Yet one I must set down.
To take away the hearth! –
Man, what greater crime?

Vacuum

As when, aged nine, not really
thinking, I dived beneath
the three-quarters unfurled

tarpaulin of a swimming pool
and, short of air, surfaced
to find between the water

and the covering only
the meagrest light, and gasped,
grasping what nothing meant,

and dived again, then mad-swam
and made it to the end,
just, you might think, unharmed.

On your pulling through

As much as we might miss
a god we can appeal to,
one at which to rant,
an equal need emerges –
that there be something to thank.

An east coast resident stays put

Crazy place to live,
in a field, on a cliff
that every year or twenty
unstitches along one edge . . .
Yet see it how I see it:

evening after evening,
considering the waves,
the field a good way up
your window. Then one morning
wake to find the grass

sits lower in the frame,
one fewer row of caravans
between the sea and yours.
To know how things will go.
In what precise order.

Woodwork

i
The tree

Gingko, declares my mother,
sat at the table thumbing,
or leafing rather, through
the tree book to discover
whose leaf it is Matilda
has brought in from the street.

And, bingo, there it is –
the self-same, ribbed, fan-shape.
And my daughter, she must think
this process simple, common –
the seeing, then recognition
of things, and so of people.

ii
The bench

My father with the pencil, me the measuring tape –
a team, in some ways – only with the last
of our four saw-cuts in the reclaimed plank
did we work out why each was angled, sloped:

we weren't square from the outset.
My father said he thought it wouldn't matter;
and given where we'd reached, I felt it better
to fix these sawn struts to the readied bench-seat

rather than protest. So then we lugged
the new bench to the hallway, where it stood,
and where it stands still, on the uneven floor –
levelly, as my father said it would.

iii
Restoration project

Small bedroom chair (Edwardian?),
curved cane seat stove in,
as if punched, once, hard.

More likely this harm stems
from someone reaching, someone
who – their whole focus on

the wanted thing – forgot,
if they had ever known,
the nature of that which bore,

even lifted them.

iv
On your cruelty

In winter, sometimes, light
reflects off snow back up to trees,
to patches, strips of bark, the cells
beneath which start to warm up, and to grow.

Which wouldn't matter only, once this happens,
they've no time to close down again
on sensing the mistake, as night comes
and the frost prepares to burst these woken parts.

I don't know if you know, or care,
but it's termed sun-scald, this phenomenon,
which leads the surface of the tree to scar
through damage to the flesh, the heart.

In nature it occurs by accident.

Playground prayer, Cherry Tree Wood

i.m. Joanna Witt

Cherry for cradles,
maple for blocks,
birch twigs for broomsticks,
alder for clogs;

mazes from box,
willow for bats,
poplar for punnets,
tool handles, ash;

sycamore violins,
carvings from lime,
walking sticks, hazel,
may they have time.

ACKNOWLEDGEMENTS

Some of these poems, or versions of them, first appeared in the
following places: the *Reader*, the *New Statesman*, *Magma*, *Obsessed
with Pipework*, coffeehousepoetry.org and panmacmillan.com.

'Playground prayer, Cherry Tree Wood' won the Alder Hey
Children's Hospital poetry competition; 'The Bench' came second
in the Edward Thomas Fellowship poetry competition.

The title of one of these poems, 'Live Company', is borrowed
(with thanks) from Anne Alvarez's book of the same name.

Thank you to Verity, and to Kate Clanchy, John Glenday,
Don Paterson, Stephen Smith and the members of the Nevada
Street poetry group for their help and encouragement
during the writing of this book.